Talking to Ghosts

by Jon Tobias

QUILLKEEPERS PRESS

Published by Quillkeepers Press, LLC
PO Box 10236
Casa Grande, AZ 85130

Dear Reader,

I unintentionally started this small collection a little over ten years ago, beginning with very angsty poems about my father. Writing about him was a way of making sense of the question, why me? Who gave me to this man, and who let me stay with him? Without going into too much detail, violent is the first word the childhood me would use to describe him if childhood me felt safe enough to say that.

Over the years, my father's health declined. He developed COPD and Alzheimer's. He was addicted to pain medicine. He was diagnosed with bipolar. Those things added up in a way that broke him down, making it hard to see him as the monster I remember him as. He became more and more human, and even more so as I wrote about him. His death is what led me to write new poems and revise old poems to be less about the hurt he caused and more about forgiveness. I was never able to tell him how he hurt me, forcing me to find forgiveness without him asking me for it.

I was 2,000 miles away the day he died, and while at the hospital, he wanted me to call. I'll never know what he wanted to say because while debating whether I wanted to make that call or not, he passed away. He died of breathing complications after an attempted Heimlich maneuver broke one of his ribs, which then punctured a lung.

As I wrote about him, the rest of my family began to find a place within the central theme of this work. We grew up poor, scared, and in need of a love we weren't always sure was there. This small collection is an exploration into forgiveness and understanding family through poems about poverty, portraits of family members, and the importance of knowing exactly how to hold someone.

Thank you for reading,

Jon Tobias

For Emily, Robert, Kimberley and Penny

Contents

III

I

Maybe It's Genetics

You held me the way a heavy book
preserves flowers between its pages.
Your fingerprints blooming on my neck in violet.
My body outlined on the wall.

You'd press so close
more than bruises
your face stained on my face.

I wear your face like a stocking pulled over my head
like the Shroud of Turin
like that's us in the mirror
not just me.
Never just me.

And that's why I need to forgive you
Because I look so much like us
that I can never forget you.

Disassociation

You died the way starving children
in UNICEF commercials die.
So far away it might not even be real.

You died
was a reel of news text
slowly disappearing into the bottom left corner of the tv screen.

The day we had you cremated
your sister announced you'd been returned to Jesus

and all I could imagine was a shopping cart
gently rolling itself back to the queue.

Hold Yourself and Your Breath
Until This Is Over

1

I wasn't there
but I imagine my brother's arms
thick as tree stumps
wrapped around my father's chest
while he choked on an oversized piece of rib meat.

I imagine the muffled pop of ribcage
before piercing the lung
as the meat rolled out
and breath filled
into the un-collapsed lung.

I imagine the desire to not let go
the embrace of those who know
they'll never see one another again.

Cheek pressed to cheek
kiss to temple
the quiet apology.

2

I was there
watching a neighbor
perform the Heimlich maneuver on my sister
while she gagged on a piece of hard candy.

His body
massive compared to hers
hovered on all fours over her.
Her back to his chest
his palm driving his fist into her belly.

The wet unending gargles
like a plunger stuck in mud
before the hard ball finally birthed from her mouth
in a pouch of spit and snot and tears.

I remember the relief
the god we thanked
and the neighbor we hugged.

3

I wish I wasn't there
in this body
as I cried over the kitchen island
and my wife held me from behind
which only made me cry harder

My dad.
My dad.
Fuck you.

It seems that it doesn't matter
how we hold each other.

Live or die after
something is always released.

Filters

I go to send a selfie
to tell my wife I miss her.

I swipe through the filters.
Teddy bear face
baby face
wide open mouth
makeup.

I stop on the aging filter
and it is my father's face
alive again

grey
balding
slightly bigger nose
leathered skin.

I loosen my lower lip.
I look around lost.

The filter doesn't include
coughed up food
and snot in our mustache
waiting to be wiped.

It doesn't include
our yellow cigarette-stained fingertips
debating on pushing the capture button.

Without warning
a passive
Okay
slips from my lips

like a man who needs the world
to ask him questions
where the answer only needs to be
Okay.

Do you want me to take your plate away?
Okay.
Do you want a shave after your bath?
Okay.

Do you want your nice shirt for dinner?
Okay.
Do you want your last meal to be leftover ribs?
Okay.

Do you want to call your son
and let it go to voice mail one last time?

Forgiveness Pt 1

I have a photo of you
with your grandson.
My nephew.

You both sit on a couch
wearing matching pajamas.
He shows you something in a book.

A big red dog, or maybe,

a bright yellow ferocious beast.
You look at the page with a big toothless smile
while adjusting your oxygen tube
with your upper arm as if it were
an unruly scarf end falling from
your shoulder.

Now that you can't bite or make fists anymore.
Now that you've packed away your belts
in a box labeled, knuckles and rugburn.

Now that the anger has left your body
it has given your face
some animal likeness to gentleness
timidity.

And now I can let go of the longing
for a love I wish I knew in exchange
for proof of its existence at all.

Talking to Ghosts

I wake to you playing by yourself
instead of guarding the door
like you often do at night.

You stand on your hind legs
begging the bookcase for attention.

Your front paws move forward through the air
to place on a waiting chest
but no one catches you.

You sit and look up into the empty dark.
You turn sideways the way you do
when pressing your ribs to my shins
to get scratched
but you are not scratched.

Instead you beg
whimper a little.

It looks like a dance
as you turn and jump and sit

in front of the bookcase
that holds a large succulent
and a small blue urn
containing my father's ashes.

Schrodinger's Urn

We have started blaming everything on your ghost.
The picture frame falling from its hook.
The car keys in the dog's toy box.
The way she cocks her head at your urn
as if she has heard someone say *treat*.
The cigarette smell that lingers in the hallway
that comes from nowhere.

Because I was 2,000 miles away when you died
and I didn't call like you asked
and never saw your body

like Schrodinger's cat
there is a version of this story where you're still alive.

There is a version of this story
where we made peace with one another
and I can talk to you through a small blue urn
inside of which you are both alive and dead.

I forgive you
and want to try this again
before it is too late.

Misread

The doctor wrote
hoarse voice
but in my skimming I read
hearse voice

and now I need to know
what sound you would have to make
so that your voice might carry the dead.

Forgiveness Pt 2

I try to remember you differently,
and tell myself that forgiveness
is as easy as retelling the story.

After you died
we gathered your things
and I placed the belts with the rugburn
in a box full of bad words
knucklebones
and hunger.

I dismantled you with love.
With photos of you with your grandson.
You and your wife in the backseat of a horse drawn carriage.
Balboa Park carousel rides
and outsmarting carnival games.

With teaching kindness backwards
but still teaching it.

Like how to perform a mercy killing
with forgiveness.

And now
the only proof of your strength
lies within the dirty handprints
I left on your silver armor
that forever gathers dust
in a room none of us go in anymore.

Forgiveness Pt 3

All that you left us
was your name

and it sits in my mouth
inedible
too big to swallow.

I drool around it
not willing to spit it out.

My eyes water
but I need to tell the room
a memory I have of you.

It takes practice
bringing people back to life
while acknowledging your own pain.

It finally comes out in a cough
a hack after a self-induced Heimlich.

And then he chased the mailman naked,
screaming, 'Give me my money.'

We laugh.
I finally allow myself to laugh.

II

A Memory of my Mother

My relationship with my mother was equally as rocky as the one I had with my father, and just like with him, I try to hold on to as many human moments as possible.

I often come back to a single memory I have of her. At the time, I was embarrassed. Now, though, I understand what she did was so human it hurts to think about. We never had money and were always short on bills and always borrowing. We had unpaid tabs at a pizza place. We had neighbors who hated us but still helped because they didn't want the kids to suffer. She pawned my things while I was in school. I would come home to gifts from my grandparents gone or games I had bought working summer jobs. For the brief period we lived in a house, because the owner took section 8, our power and water was often shut off.

Even though we had no money at all, she would always treat herself to things on the first of the month that she would have to return at the end of the month. She loved nice smells, so for a brief period, she developed an essential oils addiction which she purchased from the neighborhood Sprouts. She would ask me to drive her there in the evenings with liquor on her breath. She would tell me it was because her eyes were bad at night. I used to imagine her arguing with employees about their company's no refund policy on half used essential oil bottles. I don't know how she did it because I refused to be seen with her, but she always got her money back. I know they hated her. I know seeing her would mean a night ruined or that she'd be back to return whatever she was buying.

One first of the month, I did go in with her to shop and the employee working there made a rude comment about seeing her soon to return everything and how she didn't know why she bought stuff she couldn't afford. My mother responded, *"Sometimes I get to actually keep the things I buy. I don't always return everything. I know I can't afford it, but if I don't let myself feel like I deserve something nice, I might just go crazy and kill myself because what's the point."* A few years later, I watched her try in the entrance of the home we lived in with a piece of broken window.

I was embarrassed and hated her for what I thought of as failing as a mother, but I also have empathy for her because I, too, as an adult, know what it is like to have so little that you desperately need to feel like you deserve something nice without feeling guilty for having it.

Pinocchio Prepares
to Take Photos for Make-a-Wish

The foundation is cool against my fevered skin.
First her fingers then a sponge
pressing into my cheeks like a sculptor
who doesn't have enough clay.

I think she is trying to make me
as beautiful as she is
with her brushes and liners
lipstick and eyeshadow.

I think of watching her
do her own makeup from the doorway
and I know she'll use the green powder next
to cover how the chemo has blackened my eyes.

She tells me
I will look like a normal kid when she is finished
but I want to be pretty like her.

I say
Please paint my nails.

And she does with a top-coat.
The brush grazes the edges of my fingers
and the polish hardens there like glass.

She tells me how I said I wanted to meet Jane Seymour
because everyone says they look alike.

She says to ask the Make-a-Wish people
for her to come see us.

I tell her *Tina Turner or Michael Jackson*
Dolly Parton or Disneyland.

I lie in my bed and pretend I am at the spa with her.
I want cold cucumbers on my eyes.
I want a robe instead of a hospital gown.

She smooths blush onto my cheeks and says
I just want you to look alive for a little while.

A nurse comes with a wheelchair to
remove the IV from my wrist.

My mother lifts me from the bed
and my limbs spill over her arms
as if I were a stringless marionette
a balloon animal with bones bouncing between the knots.

As she pushes me out the door she says, *remember,*
You want to meet Jane Seymour.

Misread #2

You texted Panic Attack
but I read picnic attack

and imagined of an army of ants
launching a rebellion against potato salad

until I could feel them crawling all over my skin

Home Improvement

When the maintenance man comes
she tells me to go in my room and shut the door.

He patches the hole in the wall
that starts where the floor meets the baseboard.

We were playing soccer in the house.

Questions Asked in a Nightmare

Remember when she fell face first through the porch window
making walrus tusks from glass
Her dentures a miniature disco
Blood filling her mouth—the wrong end of an hourglass

Making walrus tusks from glass
Numbing the pain with a bucket of brandy
Blood filling her mouth—the wrong end of an hourglass
She'll tell the doctor that she is clumsy

She numbs the pain with buckets of brandy
While the kitchen is a beer bottle wind chime
She'll tell the doctor that she is clumsy
Come home and tuck us in for the night

While the kitchen is a beer bottle wind chime
Morgue is chalk outlined on the patio floor
Come home and tuck us in for the night
Cigarette children with lipstick-stained filters

Morgue is chalk outlined on the patio floor
Her dentures a miniature disco
Cigarette children with lipstick-stained filters
Remember when she fell face first through the porch window

Have You Seen This Child

I remember as a boy watching
my mother respond to ads
from people looking for the children
they gave up for adoption.

She sat in the kitchen
with a yellow legal notepad
phone cord curled
between her long fingers.

Her free hand scratching illegible
shorthand onto the paper.

She'd say
Hi.
I am calling for my mom.
Is she there?

The phone calls ending with
her half sobbing a thank you
while thumbing tears from her cheeks.

She would tell us it's important to know
where you came from
forgetting the woman who raised her.

I think of my mother
who will never know who she is
and the lives she made

and to her I say
I always know where here is.
I will always know who I am.

Sometimes the Last Thing They Wrote Is What the Suicide Note Would Have Been

I filled the fridge.

I love you.

-Mom

Misread #3

The paper said obituary
but I read orbituary

which isn't a word
but sounds like what happens
when a planet falls out of orbit with a star.

Maybe the sun stopped setting
but we were never fully left in the dark.
There was still plenty of light.

III

Holding My Nephew for the First Time

My sister says
gently
as I take him from her.

Using my bicep as a pillow
I bounce him in my arms.

Careful
she says

as if he is a collection
of detergent bubbles
about to break apart
and disappear forever.

I wipe drool from his cheek
with my thumb.

When you are born
being held wrong can kill you.

The problem is
that never changes.

My Sister's Paper Zoo

Her fingers work at small rectangles of paper
until little animals begin to take shape.

Bears with the number five
wrapping across their bellies.

Zebras lined with holographic security strips.

Little green pigs.

To save money
she names them.
She folds them into something
she'd have to kill to spend.

It's the same feeling
of not wanting to cut into a birthday cake

or the guilt of finding your favorite stuffed animal
lying in the middle of the bedroom floor.

She says a prayer while she unfurls a rhinoceros
until he is just the number fifty

until he is just gasoline
and a few groceries.

The Miracle of Poverty

I ask my sister what she wants for Christmas
and she asks me to use the money
I would spend on her for her son

and I think this must be how the miracle
of the bread and fish worked

to know you have enough
and then hand to the next
instead of eating

and so on—

Growing up poor during the holidays

instead of eating—
it's wrapping a stuffed bear
in newspaper

instead of eating—
it's a little set of Disney pajamas

instead of eating—

the feeling never leaves you
to have always had so little
that anything more is too much.

Still Life

I turn onto a street not yet blocked off
as police officers crowd a car wreck
where a person lies motionless
beneath a tarp on the ground.

My mind stops time as I turn the corner
and nothing in the world moves in my rearview.

The bystanders and their dogs
the rubberneckers watching
through the screens of their phones
the squirrels crossing power lines
all freeze as if in a quickly drawn sketch.

Still life
as in still alive.

I take the route home
with only stop signs
knowing the traffic lights
will forever stay red.

Batman with Autism

My brother holds himself with his hands on his shoulders
arms crisscrossed like ammunition belts
worn by 90's action heroes.

He comforts himself this way
standing in front of the tv
watching movies on repeat
all day long.

He perseverates
Oh shit
in different variations
as superheroes celebrate victory
as orcs and elves battle
as Ripley shouts her famous line

Take that
you bitch.

I sit on the couch watching how he holds himself
until the loud pop and glass shatter
of a car accident outside
sends us both to the window.

In the parking lot below
a woman sobs into the face
of the child she holds.

No superheroes tonight.
No clear good guys or bad guys.
No police.

Just us at the window
while he repeats

Oh shit

fingers digging into his shoulders
like Batman trying to rip off a cape
he never wanted to wear to begin with.

My Brother's Voice

is an audio book you could never finish
Bobcat Goldthwait seeing a sunset for the first time

laugh like a harmonica inhale
a high note soaked in diet coke and lithium

you can hear the pistons of his thoughts
firing through his breath

each pause the tug of a chain
dredging up memory

some phone calls I just listen to him breathe
as if checking a body for signs of life

my ear so close he could kiss
my cheek if he wanted to

he practices lullabies with me
to later sing to his nephews

his voice is an 80s metal guitar solo
that only slows but never ends

I really wish they made ghillie suits
out of teddy bears

because I don't know how to ask
for someone to hold me

my brother's voice is a prayer
translated into hungry bird song

unanswered
beautiful

Robert Ends a Phone Call

Okay. I have to go now.

I love you.

Very, very much.

Okay, wait. When are you coming here again?

And we can go to Barnes and Nobles or the comics store?

Okay. Are you going to eat now?
Are you going to have good food?

I am going to have two chicken sandwiches
with special sauce.

Do you like chicken sandwiches?
We can have them next time.

Okay. I will call you tomorrow.

Hey. Are you mad at me?

Are you proud of me?

I am proud of you.

Okay. I love you.

Until the wheels fall off?

And then you'll get out and push, right?

okay
bye
g'bye
bye, bye
Alright, bye
Okay goodnight
I love you, bye
bye
I'll call you tomorrow. I promise
bye

Present Tense

I want to speak a language that only knows
the present tense

A language without memory or hope
A language without foresight

A language where etcetera and ellipsis
end sentences instead of periods

A language where *before* only means
in front of
and *after* only means
behind

I want this to be my language
A language where people only go
but are never gone

About the Author

Holding a variety of odd jobs, from working on an assembly line, acting as a shift manager at multiple pharmacies, and offering care in a group home for adults with disabilities, Jon Tobias found that the only thing he ever wanted to be was a poet. Jon graduated from SDSU with a BA in English in 2015, and is currently attending the same college to get his MFA in poetry. He has poems published in anthologies by Quillkeepers Press, Local Gems Poetry Press, White Stag Publishing, as well as short fiction published by A Word With You Press. Jon lives in San Diego with his wife, Kimberley and their dog, Penny Lane.